Picnic *on* the grounds

Picnic on the grounds

REAPING
THE REWARDS
OF CHURCH
ATTENDANCE

JUDY CHATHAM

AMBASSADOR INTERNATIONAL
Greenville, South Carolina • Belfast, Northern Ireland

Dedicated

TO ALL WHO VALUE THE REGULAR OFFERING OF A SACRIFICE OF PRAISE TO HONOR WHAT JESUS DID AT THE CROSS, TO HONOR GOD, OUR CREATOR, WHOSE FAITHFULNESS NEVER ENDS.

Appreciation

TO FAMILY, PRESENT AND THROUGH THE AGES, WHO PLAY A HUGE ROLE IN ILLUSTRATIONS USED IN THIS MANUSCRIPT.

TO A HOST OF MINISTERS, LEADERS, MENTORS, WRITERS WHO IN LIVING OUT THEIR OWN CHRISTIAN FAITH, HAVE LED ME INTO TRUTH.

TO THOSE WHO ENCOURAGE MY WRITING MINISTRY.

Picnic on the Grounds

©2005 Judy Chatham
All rights reserved
Printed in the United States of America

Cover design & page layout by
A&E Media — Rita Blajeski

ISBN 1 932307 49 4

Published by the Ambassador Group

Ambassador Emerald International
427 Wade Hampton Blvd.
Greenville, SC 29609
USA
www.emeraldhouse.com

and

Ambassador Publications Ltd.
Providence House
Ardenlee Street
Belfast BT6 8QJ
Northern Ireland
www.ambassador-productions.com

The colophon is a trademark of Ambassador

Table of Contents

Biography ix
Introduction 1

Before the Picnic:

1. We See The Situation We Are In 7
2. We Learn How To Deal With That Situation 29
3. We Hear The Biblical Story To See
   Where We Fit In 45

At Church

4. We Look For A Workable Plan 61
5. We See How A "Good Habit" Plays Itself Out 67
6. We See What His Sacrifice Is
   And What Ours Is 81

At the Picnic on the Grounds

7. In Relationship, We See God In It All 87

Biography

Judy Chatham, a 20 year lecturer/ writing instructor at Indiana University of Indianapolis, has written three biographies and one autobiography with Christian themes and strong attention to place and local color. *A Whirlwind's Breath*, the signature of her writing career, is about living through and overcoming adversity when both of her children were seriously ill. The book with the most national attention is *Windows of Assurance*, a story about military family life and the spiritual triumphs of Billie Cash of Memphis, Tennessee. Of local interest to Indianapolis is *Papa, I Want To Be A Surgeon*—the story she worked on with a college dean at the Indiana University Medical Center. Of interest to the Memphis, Tennessee area is *The Bridge*, the story of an award winning, innovative educator in the area. In December 2004, *The Amber Necklace* was received locally as both a tool for ministry and a read aloud Christmas book at gatherings of

Picnic *on* the grounds

family and friends. Since 1999, Judy has served on a panel of judges for the annual Evangelical Press Association's Gold Medallion Award for books with a Christian theme. She and her husband are active members of Community Church of Greenwood in Greenwood, Indiana.

Note: Names and dates of people and events used in the illustrations in this book have been changed in order to protect all identities.

Introduction

This book is written for the emerging congregations of the Christian faith. It is a call to continue meeting together in a church setting even after, and especially after, a person has agreed with God that there is sin in a life, and after that person has recognized that only God has the answers to problems all of us face. Let me explain:

Seated on the second row on the aisle near the stained glass window, I looked away from our minister this Sunday morning. A narrow slant of light between the brilliant royal blue and ruby red allowed me to look out into the parking lot. This morning my mind strayed to the picnic planned at noon, but as I mentally placed the items into the picnic basket, I was jostled more than a little when I heard our minister say, "God is Love."

Today these three words rang more clearly than ever before, even though for 36 years I had heard these words stated over and over and over again. God is Love! What is love? God is Love. The essence of love is God. Loved by an earth-bound someone? God is in that love, for God is Love.

Squinting to look through the narrow pane of clear glass on this Sunday morning, I heard that God is Love. And this revelation uncovered much more. I also learned that church attendance—God's telling us not to give up meeting together—is more than a suggestion.

Not only is it a command, it is a necessity. On this day I learned that multiple applications of Truth are necessary to penetrate our finite, mortal minds. Our capacity to comprehend is also punctuated with the hammering of the popular culture that so brazenly distracts and dissuades.

Sweetly singing, "Jesus Loves Me This I Know" at age two; lovingly pasting pictures of Jesus on Vacation Bible School materials at age seven; and answering the questions correctly when joining the church at age eleven (or whenever), apparently is only the foundation of understanding. Whereas I had learned a few Bible verses, stories of Jonah and Noah, and had envisioned the huge stalk of grapes carried out of the Promised Land, I had not even begun to understand an oft-repeated phrase—God is Love.

God knows the problem and the solution. That is why he insists that we continue meeting together to sing the Truth over and over; to tap it out over and over again; to recite

introduction

it over and over again; to memorize passages of it; to hear ministers and teachers repeat the same phrases over and over again. When we say we learned it at church, the meeting house, we are talking about a level of meaning that only God can direct.

Today we see a serious departure from commitment to attending church regularly. If "Jesus Paid It All," why do I need to do anything else—like giving up my Sunday mornings in order to attend church and all that entails?

The answer is multifaceted, but when we see a community of believers huddled together in unity, we hear prayers that are not individual prayers, but rather 10 fold, 20 fold, 30 fold prayers that waft up to the presence of God. The Bible says that pleases Him, seeing His people leaning on Him. He hears and releases Holy Spirit power likewise multiplied. Into that kind of setting, He imparts truths, principles, directions, favors, blessings, and love that may have been unrecognizable for years, may never have been uncovered in the life of the individual who chooses to go it alone, not communing in the Body of Christ.

This book has grown out of a lifetime of sitting under the direction of sixteen senior pastors in various cities and countryside churches. Under some of these ministers I was either too young to understand or too removed to be receptive, but of the sixteen, I can quote specifics, in some cases—pages of specifics, I have learned from them. All of them had found

Picnic *on* the grounds

their way into the arms of God. Why? They never gave up meeting together, learning and growing together as a part of the Body of Christ.

The impact of the messages of nine senior pastors, plus, those of scores of teachers, assistant pastors, musicians molded my life and that of others to begin the journey to maturity in Christ. This book is divided into seven sections which illustrate what a person is likely to take away from that many years of listening and participating in programs and worship.

Equipping the parishioners is the business of the church. In today's multi-faceted, fast paced, 24/7 roller coaster world, being equipped cannot be taken lightly, but more important is the peace that results from the understanding that God, the Creator, and I have reached an agreement that I am His and He is mine for all time.

God is Love indeed!

Judy Chatham

Greenwood, Indiana

January 2005

CHAPTER 1

Before the Picnic: We See the Situation We Are In

An understanding of "the situation we are in" places great responsibility upon the few who understand early and can lead the rest. These people usually become Sunday School teachers like my Aunt Mildred did or wise people who sit on the front porch dispensing advice to the young and old alike. Since not every reader would know Aunt Mildred or some other wise person, I have chosen to point to the example of Nehemiah of the Bible as one who could put the puzzle of this life together and lead his people.

Picnic *on* the grounds

Nehemiah's story is universal in every way for it tells of a ritual that every contentious individual has engaged in since time began—that of staring at the ceiling trying to understand the reality of the situation, conducting the night watch:

Nehemiah, the cupbearer for a king, received word that his beloved hometown of Jerusalem was in ruins. But most important, he learned "those who survived the exile and are back in power are in great trouble and disgrace." (Note 1) The news sent him reeling, overcome with great sorrow. He felt powerless to help rebuild the Jerusalem wall that lay in rubble, powerless to help his people who had come into great trouble and disgrace. Unable to overlook such a serious dilemma, Nehemiah gathered all his assertive power, approached the king asking for permission to take leave in order to return home and assess the damage. Surprisingly, the king released him from duty, allowing him to leave immediately. Mentally preparing himself to see the first signs of devastation, he pointed his horse toward Jerusalem.

Anyone who has been told the dear ones in his or her life have fallen into trouble and ruin, has stood where Nehemiah stood. Military men of all ages can identify with Nehemiah, this able and dutiful son and brother who loved his country so much that he set himself up to sacrifice all in order to protect that country. And anyone who has returned home to a burned out shell of a house, a break-in, a splintered pile of brick and siding where the house once stood, can identify with Nehemiah.

we see the situation

He, on the one hand, happy to be home and on the other, sad to see the ruins, visited with family and neighbors, secretly shoring up strength to face the task ahead. Then, on the third night and after the family had fallen asleep, Nehemiah did what soldiers, mothers, fathers, and all caretakers have been doing for centuries—he set out upon a night watch— to assess the damage, a fact finding tour of the ruin, to discover the trouble his people were in. Under cover of darkness the evaluation began.

For the mother, the ceiling above the bed is the field of observation. Searching for answers on how to rear a child and ways to get all of the work done, Mom traces the ceiling so well she has memorized every plaster crack, every errant speck and dot on this field of observation. And so, Nehemiah, under the cover of darkness and telling no one, set out to circle the city on his horse.

First, he came to the Valley Gate, then, to the Jackal Well and Dung Gate, then on to the Fountain Gate, and on and on he rode around the city of Jerusalem. What he saw at each section of the wall was more foreboding than what he had seen at the last. The task ahead was enormous.

Night Watch. Nehemiah's discovery must have been much like that of David when he was prompted to write the 63rd Psalm:

Picnic *on* the grounds

> ...I have seen you in the sanctuary
>   And beheld your power and your glory.
> ...On my bed I remember you;
>   I think of you through the watches of the night.
>   Because you are my help,
>   I sing in the shadow of your wings.
>   My soul clings to you;
>   Your right hand upholds me....

Night. That part of the 24 hours, when, for some, sweet rest overcomes the body, for others the great anxiety, the overloaded imagination kicks into high gear.

The dots on the ceiling of my own night watches came together over a period of growing-up years. Like most young people of my generation, I, like young Nehemiah, saw in the context of my rural upbringing smatterings of the "trouble we humans are in." It appears that we are born into a world that is filled with trouble. Consequently, we will deal with that trouble and sin from birth to the grave and beyond, if we do not find one who can rescue us, can save us.

Many school day incidents in a child's growing up years point to the trouble we are in. However, one incident that occurred during my sophomore year in college revealed to me, in bas-relief and for all time, the truth about our situation, what can happen to a life when evil moves in, festers and finally boils over:

we see the situation

I had moved into the YWCA my second year on campus. Joanne, Patsy and I took the last room on the second floor hallway that ran along side an auditorium and stage. Heavy wooden French doors opened out from the auditorium directly opposite the door to our room. No doubt this exit was mandatory for a public building, for the back stairs to the fire escape was around the corner from our room and off the back stairs that ran from the third floor down to the furnace room—four floors in all. So we joked that we were at the end of the cull de sac and had more privacy than anyone in the building—unless, of course, the janitor had the "real sanctuary" with his area in the furnace room.

Eight girls and one of the housemothers lived on the second floor, which also included a large kitchen where each of us had a shelf to put our food; a laundry room; and a quiet study room. The remaining 42 girls, plus another housemother lived on the third floor, which was really the fourth floor once one counted the basement, that lower floor which housed the weight room and swimming pool of the YWCA. Approximately half of the girls were college girls with the balance making up a pool of working girls who had entry-level jobs in the corporations and downtown offices nearby.

During the daytime hours, the YWCA had non-stop traffic with little girls coming to the auditorium on our floor for their gymnastics, ballet and tap lessons. Women came for their exercise classes. Elementary and high school students were coming for swimming lessons every hour on the hour

Picnic *on* the grounds

after school until 8:00 p.m. Plus, clubs met in the downstairs meeting rooms, groups rented out the large reception area rooms for special events and dances. Plus, the boyfriends of the 50 girls upstairs came to pick up the girls for dates. Upon arrival the date would check in at the reception desk, the girl would come downstairs to the lobby; sign out with the understood promise of being back to sign in by 11:00 p.m. on week nights and 12:00 p.m. on weekend nights. These rules were rarely challenged, for the rooms at the Y were quite inexpensive, and a long waiting list sat on the administrator's desk. We could be replaced. Plus, we had great respect for the two women who were our housemothers. We really wanted them to accomplish their purposes with minimum inconvenience; therefore, we followed the rules with few reminders.

Occasionally a carload of boys would follow a group of girls home from the downtown area and block our way as we parked the car in the dark parking area at the back of the building, or they would drive behind us, all the time teasing and flirting, as we walked from downtown. Then they would park by the back door so we had to walk around their car to get to the door. We were fun to taunt and tease, and most of the young men were college students at one of the three colleges in town, one state school and two private schools. That was the extent of the danger to our lives as we came and went from the Y. Occasionally there was a lover's quarrel in the lobby or a confrontation between two boys interested in the same girl, but with fifty girls involved, these incidents were also minimal.

we see the situation

It was in the late fall when the weather had turned the days to gray and drizzle that I became bogged down in my Spanish class studies. Miss McGraph led a class of twenty students, all of whom had studied Spanish in high school. Having never taken a Spanish class before attending college, I had extra studying to do. On one particular weeknight, I set the alarm for 5:00 a.m., placed my notebook and text by the door in preparation for going to the study room before my roommates, or anyone on the hall, awoke the next morning.

While it may seem a bit spooky for me to be roaming the dark halls of the Y in the early morning, I really never thought to be afraid. Even though there was a large dark auditorium/theater, which covered the entire south side of the hallway beside our rooms, and the back door where workers and young college men entered to go to the basement to obtain working orders for odd jobs, I often left the room in my short pj's, book and notebook in hand. Today was no exception. The building was stone silent, and a bit chilly. Not even the working girls had headed for the kitchen or laundry room.

I settled in at the large round table in the middle of the study room, sitting in the straight back wooden chair with my back to the wall that ran along the stairwell that went from the basement to the third floor. It had been an hour of intense study when I noticed the time was already 5:59 a.m.

No sooner had I noted the time than my straight back chair flew straight up in the air as high as the top of the table and

Picnic on the grounds

then just as quickly dropped with a harsh thud onto the hardwood floor. Because the chair had remained upright, I remained seated for this unexpected "moving up higher." Simultaneously to the rising chair incident there was a loud BOOM!! outside the closed door, so loud and jolting that my entire body reacted, my teeth clinched to prevent the chatter that resulted. For what seemed like forever, but only minutes, I couldn't move. Staying seated suddenly seemed the best way to deal with this development outside the door. When I did rally, I could see what I thought was smoke coming under the door; in fact, I could smell smoke. The building was on fire! Quickly, I gathered my book and notebook and ran from the room, only looking back one time at the wall of smoke that had sealed off the stairwell and the entire front of the building. As I ran, I knocked on doors—first, the housemother's door; then, Joan's. Down the hallway I ran past the laundry, knocked on Carolyn and Mae's room, then the door of Jeannie and her roommate and last of all, I burst into our room jolting awake sleeping Joanne and Patsy. Since neither had a morning class on this particular day, one would think they would have been very upset at this new development. However, the look on my face and my few words of explanation told them not to argue. Quickly, I grabbed a trench coat, and we headed for the back stairs, out to the fire escape and down the metal steps to the ground. Down the alley we ran to the front of the building and across 7th Street opposite the Y.

we see the situation

Our near 100 year-old building was on fire. Ash gray smoke rolled out the front plate glass windows and the now opened front door. Behind came the second floor girls, down the back stairs, forty-two girls from the third floor, two steps at a time and clanged down the metal fire escape creating a cadence, which sounded fit for war.

Because of the time of day all fifty girls and the two housemothers had been inside the building. Surprisingly, since we had never held a fire drill or discussed escape routes, this evacuation went like clockwork. All of us blurted out the obvious questions—Where exactly is the fire? What started the fire? What if everything in our rooms is destroyed?

In our questioning, however, we failed to notice that the smoke coming from the building was not black smoke; likewise the "smoke" had seemed to dwindle even as the firemen arrived on the scene. Every emergency vehicle in the city soon merged onto 7th Street, police and fire sirens blaring, with every available ambulance following close behind. Understandably, the adrenalin had carried us out of the building and made us strong, but the sight of all of the emergency equipment caused many of us to dissolve into tears. Because I had been closest to the stairwell where the problem developed, I was the only one who had been lifted into the air by the explosion, and this deadly jolt had given me a head start at processing what was happening. By the time I stood on 7th street, I was alert to the max. We were separated from everything we owned; some of us were basically naked with

Picnic *on* the grounds

a little gauzy material draped here and there; and the yellow tape the police were wrapping around the building told me we were not going to go back inside any time soon.

As I look back over a few decades since this incident, I see that almost every tragedy has some kind of comic relief thrown in for good measure. This emergency at the YWCA is no exception. At exactly 6:00 a.m., at the moment of the explosion, two car loads of soldiers disembarked from their train at the station only two blocks from the back of our building. Trained for disaster, these young uniformed men, all of them near the ages of the fifty homeless young women, quickly moved into the area behind the yellow tape to assist in any way they could. Mysteriously however, the police and fire crew declined their offer causing them to leave the yellow taped area and turn toward us. Now out of their rescue mode, they turned into the boys they were and acknowledged their good fortune at arriving on this scene with fifty half-clothed girls before them with no place to go and hide. What is humorous for some may not necessarily be humorous for all, and when they saw that some of us were mortified, they came over and loaned us their uniform coats until the Red Cross gave out blankets. Having my own boyfriend who lived across the campus, I, on the other hand, focused on what was happening inside the front door of the building. Much low talking, and quick decision-making was taking place.

And then the announcement came. None of us could return to our rooms today. The girls' dorm just around the corner

we see the situation

from the Y had offered to house us in their recreation room, the Red Cross would supply us with necessities; the girls in the dorm would clothe us for the day.

With that announcement the reality of our separation from our possessions registered, and all of us spoke at once: "I have to have my class notes." "I have to have my keys to the office where I work." "I have to retrieve pictures of my grandmother" ...and the list went on.

Seemingly unsympathetic with every request, the police firmly pressed on by adding, "Girls, this is a crime scene. Detectives will be arriving soon. All of you will be questioned some time late this afternoon. And don't be surprised if your boyfriends aren't called in also. You are to report back to this area after lunch to learn when your appointment with the detective will be. We will get you back inside the building as soon as our investigation is complete. Now go over to the dorm and get some clothes and food for the day."

We went. Soon we were warm again, drinking hot chocolate and theorizing about what had REALLY happened on this ordinary school day morning.

Each of us was questioned. Several college boys were called in from two campuses nearby. Of special interest were the young men who were a few years older who might in some way be connected with the YWCA. Not to be overlooked were the boyfriends of late who had just broken up with some of the girls. The police asked us about all of them, but all of us agreed, "Why would the young men, newly unattached, have an axe to grind? They had just been released 'from captivity' to go on to live their promising future. Surely they were the happiest boys in town."

Finally one of the residents on the third floor who had been dating a policeman had some classified news that she could tell us if we promised not to tell where we heard it. From all indications someone had set a bomb in the basement of the Y, set to go off at 6:00 am, and set with enough explosives to level the building! The police were working on the fact that every one of us, fifty girls and two housemothers, were inside the building at the time the bomb was to explode. The person who had planted the bomb was intent on killing all of us in one explosion.

I stopped listening when she told me there had been enough explosives to level the building. What else did I need to know? Of course, we were to be torn to small pieces, powder to seed the clouds! Now I knew what had lifted my chair off the floor and set it back down. I knew why the smoke was more white than black—it was from sifted plastering and not smoke caused by a blaze.

One huge question remained: "So, why hadn't the explosion leveled the building as planned?"

The answer came from a housemother. "Apparently, someone had noticed the bomb, had noted the time for it to explode and had grabbed it up, bent over it and was running

we see the situation

out the basement door to deposit the bomb in the parking lot when it had exploded."

"Oh."

"And the one who saved us had bent over the bundle knowing that if it exploded it would rip through his body first and that action would greatly reduce its force in leveling the building."

"Someone saved our lives by giving his own life?"

"Yes."

"This person's teeth are embedded into the ceiling at the top of the third floor stairwell."

As my chair had left the floor, a person who had saved my life had been blown to fragments. As I flew table high; fragments of his body were propelled past the study room from the basement to the third floor ceiling! For one who, during the summer months, had worked beside an emergency room in a small county hospital and had seen a couple of seriously injured accident victims wheeled down the hallway to x-ray, this was unbelievable and, as my grandmother would have said, "too close for comfort."

It is strange how the mind processes such devastating news. One would suppose the heart would stop right then, just hearing what had been planned, even though what had been planned hadn't happened.

Picnic *on* the grounds

Several hours passed with no more news, classified or otherwise. Now that we knew more of what had happened, we too became very quiet, not bothering detectives with unnecessary questions. The police remained very reserved, somewhat angry, and stressed, for they knew what a blow their news would be to a residence hall of girls, and they also knew we did need to return to our rooms as soon as possible.

Finally the announcement came only a few minutes before the Associated Press news service broadcast it around the country. In terse, clipped words, a detective told us news that compounded all we had, unknown to him, gathered on our own.

"On Monday evening, November 15, Mrs. Cranfield met with the custodian of the YWCA, Mr. Jones. At that meeting she told him that in view of the tight budget for the coming year, he would not receive a raise in pay. Mr. Jones, usually known for his mild manner, became argumentative and finally accepted Mrs. Cranfield's decision, leaving the building at 9:00 p.m. Apparently, he returned home.

As well as we can piece the events of the next few hours together, some time between 9:00 p.m. and 6:00 a.m. Tuesday, November 16, Mr. Jones returned to the Y, this time, we believe he, or someone with him, came carrying a homemade bomb which, he or someone with him, planted in the basement under the stairwell."

we see the situation

There was a collective gasp as all of us whispered, "Our friend, Mr. Jones, the custodian?"

"After careful evaluation of the materials which made up the bomb, we have learned that Mr. Jones, or someone with him, had accurately estimated the amount needed to level this building. He, or someone with him, had also determined the best hour for the explosion, an hour when he, or someone with him, was assured that all of you would be inside your rooms asleep in your beds. We surmise that Mr. Jones, or someone with him, set a bomb in your residence in retaliation for the slight on the upcoming salary. Mr. Jones had been the sole custodian at the Y for a number of years, carrying the heavy load of keeping the aging building in good repair. Understandably, he had decided he was due a raise in weekly salary for his services. However, there was no money in the budget for this raise. Take note of what can happen when anger takes over the senses of one who had formerly been considered a mild mannered person."

Faces blanched to pure white, we sat quietly, not daring to look around especially not wanting to look in the direction of Mrs. Cranfield. No one moved for several minutes. Then one by one we rose and walked outside. Who wanted to go back to the rooms? We had been violated. Now we knew that our safety had never been assured. Our custodian had been the grandfatherly type who had full run of the building—harmless as a guardian to all of us. All night long he could catch glimpses of us running down the halls, of the girls dancing the twist and the hula in the auditorium across the hall—doing all of the harmless girl-fun-things that any one of us would have done in front of our fathers or our brothers. Mr. Jones had not been in the category of father or brother however. He had set out to murder us. And his method—he wanted us blown to bits.

Hour by hour the mind played on. Who was this evil person we had come to trust with our lives? His gentlemanly greeting, his humble manner created a façade behind which he could hide a smoldering hatred of us. Secretly, he had envisioned limbs, tissue, hair flying through the air.

"But he changed his mind," my friend Karen, who lived in the dorm across the street, quietly reminded me. "He was going to commit an evil deed, but he changed his mind. Have you ever wanted to do something against the rules, and then changed your mind and didn't do it? While the enormity of this deed surpasses all you and I have invented, the principle is the same: He was going to do it—but he didn't."

I had one more question: "Which do you suppose happened—did God save us by entering his body and walking him out the door, bomb in hand? Or—did Mr. Jones make a conscious decision that took his life, but may save his soul for all time?"

Quietly we pondered that thought. Then both of us came to the same conclusion, "We'll never know."

we see the situation

All in all, that experience in my young years gave me a picture of the extent of the problem we humans face. In a very short time we can become insane with anger, rage, to the extent that we could commit the ultimate crime—the murder of a human being.

One can argue that my example of the human condition is a bit extreme. Not every day do people set out to bomb buildings full of innocent people. No. That is true. But every day honest family women and men go to work to earn an honest wage, and every day the income barely meets the payment of the bills. When salary increases are overlooked, and the employee feels taken advantage of, anger results. The result of escalating anger can be disastrous.

And, of course, there are many examples of lives that are in trouble and lie in ruin. The conclusion remains the same, no matter which example we choose, we are unable to do anything in this often disappointing life in an honorable way without the help of God who can save us, and often does save us from daily trouble, not to mention, disaster—as well as for all eternity.

As the reel of my night watch experiences plays on, I remember long nights in the hospital rooms of more than one hospital. Every night for twenty-two nights I heard the click of the monitor either attached to the dwindling IV drip or the blood transfusion, or chemotherapy. I heard the nightly buzz of the nursing staff in the hallway of the children's hospital. The scene takes place during the month of the diagnosis of leukemia in our son. I watch as the precious formula of powerful drugs promises life itself once it hits the veins of our fourteen-year-old.

My mind whirls with the flash of lights on the helicopter pad on top of the opposite wing of yet another hospital eight years later. It is the night after the late afternoon emergency brain surgery to relieve the pressure caused by "an impressively large frontal lobe tumor" in our second son.

Night watch. Those hours when one fears that the doctors of the world may be flying to some far away medical conference; the emergency room staffs may be less than up to par; plus, the police and fire crews might be busy elsewhere should you call for help.

Night—that time of the 24 hours when body temperature elevates only to remind you that your brother-in-law died of a high fever that couldn't be relieved even after his body had been packed in ice.

Night—that time when you must work things out. It is ground zero where the bottom line must be interpreted in preparation to tackle the problems of the day ahead.

And so, Nehemiah collected his data, all the while planning what he would need to do to restore the wall to its former glory. Stifling sobs, yet planning. These two ingredients of many a night watch continue yet today… putting one foot in front of the other, yet sobbing with every step.

we see the situation

The situation we are in is bleak without the presence of someone to save us. The Bible says that Savior is Jesus, who died for the sins of the world over two thousand years ago, the one who offers His salvation freely to all who will receive it.

Having lived many years trying to make sense of the situation we are in, I have concluded that to know more about this saving grace and this Savior, to learn about Jesus and what He has done for us is to attend church services where the gospel is unfolded week by week. That sounds like a simplistic solution to a huge problem. Yes, but God attends church services too, and with His power to whisper answers into the quieted and prepared heart, the solution sounds full of promise.

What is the reason for such urgency? I believe the story of the rage of the custodian answers that question better than any explanation I might give. Here we had a respected gentle person, a leader of his church, a family man, a hard worker who in an unguarded moment filled with rage that swallowed up his reputation and moved him to commit an act of disastrous proportions.

Urgency is a theme that runs throughout the Bible. Why? Because we plan our best plans, and our best may not include all that will come our way. Our times—we do not know. And—that is the situation we are in.

Journal Reflections on Chapter 1:

1. Put into words the reality of the dilemma you faced when you were born into this world.

2. What arrangements have you made for living in peace, living the abundant life here, for all time and eternity?

3. Tell how you identify with the idea that everyone has, at one time or other, conducted a night watch, after everyone else in the house is quietly resting?

4. Just as one of the major defining moments in my life came to light in the story of the custodian's revenge at the YWCA, tell of your own defining moment that revealed the depth of the trouble you or anyone else could be in with very little prompting.

5. It appears that sobbing and planning are strange companions; yet have you ever seen them working together in your own life?

Chapter 2

Before the Picnic: We Learn How to Deal with that Situation

At first glance, many options to dealing with the problem we find ourselves in abound. Many would challenge my premise that church attendance provides the fastest and the most sound way to deal with the problems we are in. One could anesthetize oneself with daytime drugs and nighttime sleeping medication. One could become a runner and run so many miles a week the euphoria of the runner's high would squelch the pain of the problem. Work could be the solution—bumping up the workweek to 70+ hours of work. One can find a new marriage or business partner, a new willing ear to sympathize and comfort. The creative person can find all types of diversions. The addictive types can rely on their first loves. But soon, one by one, the options dwindle and finally comes the day—usually the day the problem has escalated beyond recognition—that is the day when the one who conducted the night watch, assessed the problem and enlisted a way to overcome it, runs out of ideas, solutions and reaches the end of all strength.

Through several years of attempted "wall building for the trouble we are in," many have learned there is only one constancy that works. Also, they have found that the best way to tap into that constantly abiding source is to run toward the church. The biblical story we heard in childhood, the story of Jesus as Savior, One to save us from everything including ourselves, is no myth—and, for most of us, we heard it at church.

When I was a child I observed adults attempting to make amends with a God for whom they held at least a distant affection. After years of neglecting the church in their community, they became weary. They decided to go out, like Nehemiah, assess the damage and restore their abandoned church, or in this case the church building, to its former glory:

EASTER SUNRISE AT FAULKNER CHAPEL

Daddy was remembering. I could tell. Faulkner Chapel was one of the six country churches on the 1950s Methodist charge in Maxwell and Northeast Townships in Raglan County, Indiana. Daddy must have visited this church be-

deal with that situation

fore. While he looked the place over, I arranged dolls Connie and Betsy on the dusty church pew and told them not to make a sound.

"The preacher is speaking," I whispered.

Of course, I was that preacher, and my subject of the sermon: "Don't Sing Unless You Mean It!"

My sermon being short, and my Daddy's inspection being long, I went outside to hunt some mushrooms—little honey-colored morels hiding around the crumbling foundation of the old building. As usual, mushrooms hid from me. Only when Daddy walked with me did I ever find one.

On the way home I learned why we were checking out the old church building. Two nights before, a couple of men had stopped by our house and had asked Daddy to join them in an effort to clean up old Faulkner Chapel, and get it painted before Easter Sunrise service. Mr. McLaughlin had told them they could empty last year's corn crop, remove the hay and have the one service before he hauled in this year's crops. Rev. Porter, pastor of the active churches on the charge, was leading this effort.

On the way home after this initial visit, Daddy turned to me and proudly announced, "We're going back into the old church one more time and have Easter Sunrise service. Grandmother will play the pump organ, and everyone will be there."

Picnic *on* the grounds

A few weeks later, I tagged along with Connie and Betsy and watched as the men set up their tall ladders to paint the inside of the church. Because of sentimental remembrances, they decided not to paint the front wall where the mural was. Some of the women would roll clay over it instead and not disturb the fading pastels.

One night the men removed the two Warm Morning heating stoves that faced each other in the middle of the room. They closed up the holes in the walls where the stovepipes connected to the chimney. Black dust rolled. The next night they began to paint. Every few days the women from the other churches and around the countryside went before the painters, removing layers of cobwebs, wiping out the windows, spraying the crevices where the wasps lived. Finally everyone pitched in to wash down the pews. Loretta said, "This could go on forever. The more dust we wipe up, the more we find."

One evening the men decided to get up into the belfry and try to get the old church bell in working order for the Easter service. Climbing straight up, no incline at all, one of the men took on the task. After swinging the rope over the rung of the ladder several times, he freed the old cast iron bell so that the clapper could clap its message…Come to Church…Come to Church….Yelling down from the belfry to the men below, the retriever announced—"Do we make it toll or do we swing it from side to side?" This bell ringing was a high point of the clean-up job. People all around heard the practice bell and knew the church was now ready for the sunrise service.

deal with that situation

Even though Rev. Porter was the leader of the restoration group, there were just as many as he who were passionate about this project. People who had never attended church services there in the old days wanted to enjoy this experience of reliving history by seeing the old church opened again on Easter morning.

The whole countryside was abuzz about this transformation. People dropped into the country stores up the road, first at Oscar's and then at George's where owners furnished a day-by-day report on the project. Even when the men went in to inquire about the spring turkey season, they always asked about old Faulkner Chapel. When anyone asked about HER, it was as though she were an old lady down the road, in need of a cleanup for Spring, an old lady in need of some rouge on her cheeks, powdered and puffed.

Finally the men and women had made good what was formerly falling apart.

Soon Easter Sunday morning came around. Normally, at our house, we set the alarm for 4:30 a.m. in order to get to the service on time. It took some time to get into that spring finery which we wore for the first time each Easter. Each year when the early alarm sounded, I was certain we had made a mistake. Looking out, I knew it must be the middle of the night instead of early morning. Yet, soon I could see the sun peeking through, and could also see the cows wandering in the pasture ready for their day to begin.

Picnic *on* the grounds

This year Karen and I wore our new blue taffeta dresses with the v-shaped inset of lace at the neckline. Mother had made the dresses from some blue taffeta curtain panels. Karen had the baby-sized version of my big blue taffeta dress. Karen was only six years old to my ten. Grandmother had bought us new white stockings and white patent slippers. Finally dressed, we sleepily dragged ourselves to the car, and as we turned west from our driveway, we could see a pink and yellow glow to the east from our rear view mirror.

First, we turned south at George's store and headed to the Sargent community down the road. Yet just as we reached Sargent we turned onto a very narrow gravel road. Karen, looking out her window, and I, looking out my window, watched as Daddy drove the car down the narrow road until we came to a turn onto a clay road, a road with a washboard of gullies running right down the middle of it. Under the arching trees, our car rolled down the now familiar hill until the road came to an opening, Daddy turned up what looked like a dirt bank, and there it was—Faulkner Chapel—with cars parked every which way out front. We pulled right under the little cedar tree at the top of the bank.

The car had barely rolled to a stop when Karen and I jumped out. Not waiting for Mother and Daddy, we gingerly tiptoed through the thick brier vines that had taken over the once grassy knoll.

deal with that situation

Every step was hindered by a brier vine, and of course, I had to stop to pick a cocklebur out of my new white stockings. None of this was of much concern because what I saw through the open doors of Faulkner Chapel was worth the fight with the brier patch.

There she was—my grandmother. She was practically standing up to put all her weight on the keys and pedals of the old pump organ. In the morning light I saw the dust flying out with each pouf of the pump.

On Easter Sunrise in Raglan County, Indiana, everyone knew the exact format of the service. We were to go inside. We would find in each pew the latest funeral parlor fan, placed there for the coming summer months, all new and ready for the upcoming hot weather. We would look around to see new Easter hats, and then the service would begin. Taking up our hymn books, which had been carried in from one of the active churches down the road, we turned to the well-known Easter songs. Funny that we needed books, for everyone knew the three songs the people of this area have been singing since time began—the three songs everyone expects to sing on Easter Sunday morning: "He Lives," "Up From The Grave He Arose," and "In The Garden."

I remember that this particular morning, my sister and I were grinning, as though we really understood the whole dynamic of this restoration project, not to mention the Resurrection itself. Grandmother was playing the organ as loudly as the bellows would allow, Karen and I were singing as loudly as we could to reciprocate. Soon we came to verse three of "He Lives," when Karen sang, "Stand up, stand up, O Christian, lift up your jaws and sing…."

"Jaws?!"

That was too funny to let go. Jaws? What would mother say? We were supposed to be serious. This was Easter Sunrise Service, the holiest time of the year. My giggle caught Karen's attention, and she began to giggle, not knowing why, but not wanting to pass up an opportunity to giggle.

Fortunately, Mother and Daddy were busy singing as loudly as they could and missed the fact that I had elbowed Karen so we could share our private joke. Soon the "eternal hallelujahs to Jesus Christ her King" pulled us back on track.

As the preacher told us about Jesus coming out of the grave and being seen in the garden, I surveyed the walls of the old church and looked for all of the plaster patches Daddy had told us about. I couldn't help but marvel that even as we sat there a stream of sunlight fell across my legs and wonder of wonder, there remained some dust to dance in that light. Loretta had been correct; the dust was reproducing.

I looked around at the people making sure they were hearing my Grandmother play the song as the offertory was taken. I realized that I didn't know many of these people, but somehow, it didn't matter because we were having a church party

deal with that situation

this morning. Soon we had the closing song—yes, it was "I come to the garden alone, while the dew is still on the roses." Sure enough the roses were there. One of those wild rose briers had wrapped itself around my new stockings the minute my feet had left the running board of our Plymouth.

After the benediction, neighbors, lingering longer than usual, greeted one another hanging onto every last minute in the old church. By now the sun was bright as noon-day, and stomachs were growing hungry for breakfast. Families told one another where to meet for breakfast. Finally most of the drivers had figured out how to get turned around and down the bank of the dirt road.

Meanwhile, Karen and I were hanging close to Grandmother because we were proud of her being the one to provide all the music, but we had another motive for following her around as she gathered up her things to leave. We knew she had two large Easter baskets for us, complete with chenille baby chicks and a tall swath of pink see-through wrap over the whole basket. It didn't hurt to start thinking about such things now that the Sunrise Service was over.

Grandmother and Rev. Porter met in the room near where the two old Warm Morning stoves would normally have greeted each other in the middle of the floor. She and Rev. Porter glowed as they talked about what a wonderful morning all of us had No sooner had they said that than Mr. McLaughlin entered one of the two front doors of the church and jovially

Picnic *on* the grounds

bounded down the aisle, coming straight for the preacher. Karen and I took it all in as he said, "Rev. Porter, I need the keys. Tomorrow she's going to be a corncrib again, and I'll put my hay over there."

His words lingered in the air, as first Grandmother, then the preacher, then Karen and I turned to see just where that hay was going to be dumped. You could have heard a mouse tiptoeing across the polished floor. Not one of us had a word to say.

With our upbringing of hearing stories of the hardworking farmers in the area, we knew that it was only right that Mr. McLaughlin should have his church/ barn back. After all, he had bought it from the church organization several years ago. Resigned to what had to be, Rev. Porter slowly pulled the keys from his suit pocket and handed them to Mr. McLaughlin. Grandmother got busy with her own car keys as she did when she wanted to avoid something. And Karen and I began to think of that big Easter basket that awaited us.

Mother and Daddy had gone on home after Karen and I had begged to ride with Grandmother. Once we were in the backseat of her old orange and crème-colored Dodge, we turned and looked out the rearview window, looking at Faulkner Chapel down at the bottom of the hill. It looked smaller and smaller as Grandmother steered her big car up the hill to finally make the turn on to the county gravel road.

deal with that situation

All I remember about our ride to the corner where we turned at the store and then as we passed Grandpa's gate, were these words, "Judy, they had good intentions. Everyone wanted to make Faulkner Chapel like it used to be, if only for one day… Yes, you're right, it will never be a church again."

That evening as I lay sleeping, I dreamed about the church. The dream came into focus with me and my two dolls sitting on the back pew, when we heard Mr. McLaughlin's pickup truck grinding its heavy self up the dirt bank and backing to the front door.

Down the road from the church the farmers paused and leaned on their hoes as they watched Mr. McLaughlin shovel the grain out of his truck and on to the newly polished floors. Women cranked up their telephones and called the neighbor ladies across the field from them.

"I sewed that cushion for the preacher's chair so he wouldn't tear his pants on a splinter."

"Yes, I washed those windows almost every week for two months, trying to get the layers of cobwebs out and the sunlight in."

"I had such a feeling of peace in there last Sunday morning."

"Well, in spite of it all, I'm glad I cleaned that mural. I think God was proud of me for all that work."

And so it was in the hollow area of limestone country where the McLaughlins, the Sandifers, the Arnolds, the Browns, and the Tuckers lived.

Picnic *on* the grounds

Resigned to the fact that every man must do what he has to do, they quietly watched as Mr. McLaughlin reclaimed his barn. Before the week was out, they could see the corn resting against the windowpanes from which that Easter morning sun had danced onto the polished floor. Helplessly, traveling by in their wagons and cars, they turned away, rode the ruts of the dirt road that rounded the wildflower-laden church yard, looking straight ahead, they headed toward the store where they could trade their eggs for the weekly stock of groceries.

So quietly did the neighborhood return to what it had been before the restoration of Faulkner Chapel, I rarely heard a word about the place in the years that followed. Yet, I do recall one old saintly lady saying, "Life is nothing more than a series of giving up what we want to keep." She didn't say she was talking about Faulkner Chapel, but since it had been one of my losses, I thought she must have been talking about wanting to keep the country church below the hill.

When Faulkner Chapel closed as a church and became a corn crib, the people of at least three generations who lived in the valley around the church building lost all of the benefits of coming together and calling themselves the Body of Christ.

After witnessing this attempt by the parishioners at Faulkner Chapel to reconcile with God's original purpose for that building, I moved on through life to have a number of experiences of my own choosing—attempts to locate that Savior I felt I had once had and had now lost. Fortunately, the

deal with that situation

one pattern in all of my search—I always turned toward the church (the physical shell as well as the people who make up the church) and not away from it.

Journal Reflections for Chapter 2:

1. As you reflect on your past, what methods have you used in your own life to deal with the situations) that came your way?

2. As you read about the efforts of the people in the Faulkner Chapel community, what were your thoughts?

3. Like the Faulkner Chapel neighbors, what attempts, successful and unsuccessful, have you made in seeking the Savior?

Chapter 3

*So — Before the Picnic:
We Hear the Biblical Story to See
Where We Fit In*

A summary of the story, which tells me where I fit in:

> You hear of wars and rumors of war —
> War in the East and War in the West,
> But there's really just one war going on,
> A major conflict declared eons ago —
> A war between God and Satan.

Picnic *on* the grounds

After Michael and his angels fought
Against Satan and his angels,
Satan lost the battle.
As a result, God told Satan
There is no place here for you.
If he could be GOD,
Which he wanted,
Satan could get revenge
By destroying God's seed—
mankind.

It was in the Garden of Eden
That Satan began his work
By planting the idea for the fall
Of Adam and Eve.
And, as a result,
Paradise was closed to Adam
And Eve for all earthly time.

Yes, there is still a war going on,
Yet, Satan doesn't fight from heaven anymore,
Nor does he wage his battle from hell.
No, he fell into the formless void
Out of which God made the earth.
When he saw that God was creating

where we fit in

Man to inhabit the earth,
Satan sat up his seat of power here.

God, of course, is not surprised by all of this—
For even before the foundation of the world,
God devised a war plan to defeat Satan;
He would allow man to have Free Will.
Man would be placed
Right in the middle of the battleground
Near Satan's own power structure.
In the Garden of Eden,
Man failed his first of many tests.
From that point on,
Satan continued to deceive man.

In fact, during Noah's time
Satan succeeded in deceiving the whole world,
Only eight souls were saved.
Then Satan continued by deceiving whole nations—
Egypt, Sodom, Gomorrah, and for a season, Israel.

From days of old, God placed his hand on Israel
And Satan noticed.
The Lord performed supernatural works for his people,
Delivered them with miracles,
Gave them great revelations of his love.
Consequently, after the Exodus,

Picnic *on* the grounds

Satan incited rebellion and idolatry in Israel.
Finally, when the time came to enter the Promised Land,
Only Caleb and Joshua escaped Satan's deception.
The battle was going Satan's way.
It seemed every battle was going his way.
He overtook the Babylonians, the Philistines,
Moabites, Hittites, Canaanites, and the Northern Kingdom.
Finally, Satan set his sights on the surviving Children of Israel.

He introduced demonic worship of Baal,
Asteroth, and Molech,
And the Israelites continued to reject God,
the Holy One.
These Children who had watched their parents succumb
To horrible deaths, had gone from funeral to funeral
Yet, they still turned to demonic idol worship.

For centuries afterward
Satan continued to fight victoriously;
He possessed the minds of King Ahab,
Jeroboam and Manasseh.
Finally the Book of Judges closed with these chilling words,
"Every man did that which was right in his own eyes."
Satan had succeeded
In making the worship of God irrelevant
Each one, in his own way,

where we fit in

Interpreted the Word and the Law.
But the Lord God was not concerned about Satan's victories,
For he already had a war plan in motion.

In the fullness of time,
God sent his Son to the battlefield.
God in the flesh
Entering the battle himself.
God was putting Satan on notice,
This action was God saying—
"The victory is mine."

When Jesus' birth took place in Bethlehem,
The announcement sent shudders
Through Satan's camp.
"This is God's son!" the demons cried.
In desperation, Satan's emissaries
In an attempt to kill Jesus, the Son
Killed every male child under age two.

At His chosen time,
God planted a cross
Right in the middle of the battlefield,
On the cross God placed his Son.
Jesus' blood spilled down on the field
Drop by drop.
It began to wash away the sins of mankind.

Picnic on the grounds

"It is finished," Jesus cried.
Satan and his demons trembled and quaked,
Realizing the battle was over.
"Our power over mankind is broken!"
Three days later
Another powerful cry—Christ is risen!

What was the power that Satan lost that weekend?
The power to accuse anyone
Who has been cleansed by the blood of Jesus.
The chains of guilt, fear and condemnation were broken
Satan was robbed of all his power to deceive and destroy
Those who live by faith in Jesus' sacrifice.
In the war,
One kingdom is dark, the other—
The kingdom of light.

Satan now knows he has a short time
This short time began at Calvary.
Since then—
Satan has grown exceedingly more incensed.
Daily he tries to drown the bride of Jesus Christ—
The overcoming remnant—
Every person throughout history who has
Made Jesus—Lord.
Yet when Satan touches God's own—
He touches the apple of God's eye.

where we fit in

As for Satan's last ditch effort—
He's releasing everything in his arsenal
To bring down God's elect.
If the love of money grows cold,
Satan orders—
"Strike them with senseless sensuality!"
"Take over the media!"
Fill everyone with lust!"
Attack the children with images
They cannot erase from their minds!"
"Wash God's name from every aspect of society!"

And what is God doing?
He's at work writing his law on the hearts of the young.
He says, "I'm going to end this battle soon."
I'll make short work of it all.
He waits for the last of the harvest to be gathered in;
He sees the coming harvest of the latter rain—
The underground church
To millions of communists in China;
The fall of the Iron Curtain;
Radio and television satellites beaming
The Good News into Islamic countries,
And to voodoo-worshiping islands.

With one quick stroke
God will end it all—

Picnic *on* the grounds

The Apostle John foresaw that day
When the Lord came forth to speedily
Make quick work of this end:
I saw heaven standing open, and
There before me was a white horse,
Whose rider is called Faithful and True.
With Justice he judges and makes war.
His eyes are like blazing fire,
And on his head are many crowns.
He has a name written on him that no one knows
But himself. He is dressed in a robe dipped in blood,
And his name is the Word of God.
The armies of heaven are following him.
Riding on white horses,
And dressed in fine linen, white and clean.
Out of his mouth
Comes a sharp sword
With which to strike down the nations.
He will rule them with an iron scepter.
He treads the winepress
Of the fury of the wrath of God Almighty.
On his robe and on his thigh
He has his name written:
King of Kings and Lord of Lords.

—Revelation 19:11-16 (NIV)

where we fit in

> And where will I be
> When God strikes this quick end?
> Planning and scheming to make my fortune?
> Entertaining myself on my fifth annual vacation?
> Washing God's name from the courthouse tablet?
> Or huddled in the cleft of the Rock?

(Based on a writing of David Wilkerson from his newsletter of Jan. 2004)

I don't really think my own parents wondered about where I would fit into the story of the Bible when they took me to church, they just knew I needed to be there. As a result, I sat through many services in which I had little idea of what the sermon meant. On the other hand, I sat through many where I picked up bits and pieces of information that, today, remain a part of my understanding of what it means to be a part of a church.

Note the progression of my childhood thoughts as I learned what church attendance was all about:

> *Grinning or even looking at each other mischievously is not a good thing when you are in church.*

> *The altar is made of special wood, and is the most important place in the church. Yet, the altar is just high enough for me to jump over as we play after the service is over.*

> *(a mixed message, perhaps)*

> *Since children always march into the church building to the tune of "Onward Christian Soldiers," we must be soldiers in the army of God.*

Picnic on the grounds

God's women are beautiful and his men are always handsome and are often warriors.

Quilting and God's women are almost always linked. (Thus, the quilters in the church basement)

Church plates are two inches thick and are unlike any others in the whole world.

A picture is worth more than words—we learn the Bible best with flannel graph pictures and big posters showing the Israelites carrying the Ark toward the Promised Land.

"Almost Persuaded" and "Just As I Am" are always closing songs, never openers.

Forefathers—all who went before us—are very important. Their names are inscribed on our church windows.

There is history in a church—ours had a Civil War chest holding the flag made by the church women during the years of that war.

Ministers are special people. Different. And they get pumped up right before they start to give their sermons.

Church is important because even the school children from the elementary school come across the street to our church for special Christmas and Easter programs during school hours.

Music has the power to make people happy or to make them cry.

Lorena sings louder than anyone else in the church.

where we fit in

Some people love to argue about the Scriptures.

There are leaders and there are followers in this world.

People of the church who have no children of their own love to have you come to their house. Having a child makes people happy.

Marriage is forever.

Elderly people are to be respected—Uncle Ben Allen, Mrs. Sorrells, and Mrs. Ragsdale, for sure.

A Bible quiz is an excellent competition to help one learn what the Bible says.

About ten little Bible Stories are stories that everyone knows, even adults.

Red, and yellow, black, and white—they are precious in his sight; Jesus loves the little children of the world.

Heaven is a real place. We heard about it in the hymn, "In The Sweet By and By."

Hell is real too. The Old Scratch (as Grandmother called Satan) sometimes sits on my shoulder.

When someone is sick, it is good to slip an apple pie inside the screen door and run to the car lest you disturb their rest.

1/10th of one's income belongs to God. The rest is his too, but we can keep it for now.

Picnic on the grounds

It may be that in God's plan, I have a special Bible Verse for life. The minister thought mine might be Isaiah 58:11 "The Lord will guide you always; he will satisfy your needs in a sun-scorched land and will strengthen your frame. You will be like a well-watered garden, like a spring whose waters never fail." (That early selection remains my life verse.)

What God speaks to you, you never question.

People who reject God, finally end up with hardened hearts.

There's something important about Baptism, gathering at the river that flows from the throne of God.

The rainbow is a very good thing.

God keeps a big book with my name in it. When I am bad, he writes down the date and what I did. When I am good, he does the same.

Having the ox in the ditch and being unable to attend church is a highly debatable subject.

A question we never heard at our house: Will we attend church this morning?

Death is always just around the corner. Any day could be the last.

Singing alto makes for a very pretty song, and several flats in a musical score make prettier harmony than music with many sharps.

Church people like macaroni and cheese and other fun foods.

where we fit in

Some people have the gift of finances.

Some people's lips are sealed—they never tell anything they hear.

The parsonage should be clean, for cleanliness is next to godliness.

John Wesley was a great man; great also was songwriter Fanny Crosby.

Hopefully very soon the Spirit will move us. (My grandmother had adopted the phrase: "I suppose you will sit there until the Spirit moves you." She said that to the grandchildren often. She also said it when she knew some adult wasn't doing his or her share of the work.)

While many of these seemingly immature assessments of what church is all about border near inaccuracies, they were early conclusions my young mind and heart drew regarding being a part of a church. Early conclusions, thankfully, go on to maturity.

Once again, it appears that becoming like Christ doesn't take place in one day. A lifetime of hearing God's message from every God-inspired resource is required. In our world, the church provides the majority of these resources to move us from babyhood to maturity in the ways of God.

Journal Reflections on Chapter 3:

1. As you read the summary of the story of the Bible, what did you learn about the war going on—the battle for your soul and mine?

2. What specific things did Satan do to deceive the Children of Israel?

3. How does it comfort you to know that God is not surprised by the trouble in the world?

4. When on the cross, Jesus said, "It is finished." What was finished?

5. Today and every day, what does Satan try to do?

6. Meanwhile, what is God doing?

7. If you attended church as a child, during your early years in church, what are five notions that were undoubtedly formed then and there?

Chapter 4

At Church We Look for a Workable Plan

After many decades of trying to work through the trouble we are in, I have concluded that the ladder to all successful wall building against the enemy must include regular church attendance.

What? Simply going to church week after week after week...? Simple as it may seem, there are scores of people who seemingly would try just about anything to avoid church attendance. Therefore, it must not be a simple solution at all.

Picnic *on* the grounds

According to George Barna, *The Moody Magazine,* July 2003, the following are the reasons that people give for not attending church services:

>1. We need our down time.

>2. We believe we are saved by an earlier experience and don't need to attend.

>3. We aren't joiners. We have great family and friend relationships.

>4. We see the church members living like the devil.

>5. We don't see the message of the church as relevant or intelligent in the world today.

George Barna responds to these results of his survey by adding, "Formerly the church had a stronger influence on American life and culture than anything else in the world. Today, movies, television and music have the greatest influence on American life and culture. After those influences come—the internet, books, public policy, family and school."

So why would one need to physically walk through the doors of a church and become a part of the body of Christ? Why not attend neighborhood Bible Studies on Mondays, listen to the tapes of the great Christian expositors of today, discuss issues from the Scriptures with neighbors and call for prayers *a workable plan*

of those who regularly engage in such intercession—all the while staying quietly on one's own street, attending to one's own concerns and listening to the sounds of silence? Or, in the view of others who shun the church, disassociating with the more vocal of the often less than intelligent Christians of today, staying home, even on Easter Sunday and Christmas Eve, being true to and drawing from your own private beliefs. What is so important about entering brick and mortar? After all, we carry Jesus in our hearts. Does not spiritual life transcend all that is physical in this world? And—the Bible is clear on what one needs in order to have eternal life—believe in Jesus and confess sin, asking forgiveness.

Why does one need to head out to a church in time of crisis, or any other time, when what one really needs is quiet and comfort and private times with God?

Journal Reflections on Chapter 4:

1. What, in your estimation, is the main reason people give for not attending church services?

2. Which of the reasons you mentioned, can you identify with?

3. What in your circle of friends and acquaintances appears to have the most influence on a life today?

Chapter 5

At Church We See How a "Good" Habit Plays Itself Out

"I was glad when they said unto me, let us go into the house of the Lord." Psalm 122:1

Two incidents helped me to run toward the church when I was in that transitional period when it became my turn to make my own decisions about what I would do with what Jesus had done for me. In Chapter 5, I will discuss the first of these incidents:

On an ordinary afternoon in the week when my future husband and I were packing to leave for our freshman year in college, I was sitting at the kitchen table in the home of my

Picnic *on* the grounds

boyfriend, visiting with his mother. Out of the blue (for me) and well-rehearsed (for her), she said to me, "I need to tell you something because I know this is a time when you, Barry and his twin brother could abandon all ties to the church and go your own way. Since the girl in any relationship always determines how things will go (one of her favorite lines), I feel I must caution you about this matter. Attending church is a habit, a very good habit. It, of course, becomes more than a good habit as time goes on, but for now think of it as a very good habit that will serve you well all of the days of your life. You will find that as you listen to the minister, you will come away with truths that will help you in your college life. All three of you will be leaving your childhood church where everything about regular attendance is comfortable, and you must immediately find a new church near the college campus and attend it faithfully. There will be times when you question this, but believe me, I've been over some difficult times (a son had died unexpectedly only three years earlier), and I know for sure this is truth I speak. You lead the way, and the boys will go with you."

I must say that what she was telling me, I had heard before, but nonetheless, having it come from her made a strong impression. It is as though someone must come along and put the final stamp of approval on a principle or a Truth for us to really "get it." It is true that I came to that time with a sterling record, for I was a devout Christian from early childhood to these college years. I had a healthy fear that if I disobeyed what I had learned to be the Truth I would soon be reaping

good habit plays itself out

the consequences of that deliberate act here and for all time. Besides, my parents and my grandmothers had painted a picture of the Book of Life that has a page in it solely for me. I wanted that page to reflect only the good from Miss Judy. Anyway, after my boyfriend's mother's well-rehearsed talk with me, I could say that all I had been taught melted into what she was saying and with purity of motivation I trotted off to church and never looked back, but the purity-of-motivation-part would not be true.

Immediately, I did locate a church of my boyfriend's denomination. Plus, a retired minister's wife from my own denomination and local congregation wrote to the minister of the church closest to the campus saying, "We have a wonderful girl coming from our congregation. You will want to meet her as soon as she arrives on campus and welcome her to your church." That campus minister kindly responded with, "Esther, I know this girl is as wonderful as you say and I will be looking for her when she arrives, but first, I need to know her name!"

Yes, we were on our way to making the smooth church transition—but my motives were less than pure. This boyfriend was going to be the husband of my dreams. If his mother had asked me to swim Indiana's Wabash River I would have—gladly. If I pleased his mom, thus having her blessing, she would encourage him to marry me, this wonderful Christian girl who would make him a perfect wife! And so, we headed off to church.

Picnic *on* the grounds

For the next twelve years we struggled with why we needed to attend church. No, it didn't take us twelve years to get the four year degree, but it did take us twelve years to be convinced that the only way one walks with the Creator who knows all things, and is in all things, is to regularly attend church services with all of the beneficial programs attached.

Let me outline that twelve-year track record in a short summary:

First, we attended the Methodist Church at the corner of campus for the morning service and attended the Baptist Church two blocks to the southwest for the evening church young people's group. The enticement for the morning service became the preaching of the great Rev. Bigler, a communicator of the gospel like few others of his time. The enticement for the evening activities was the free food, which, for the guys, would replace the lack of the Sunday evening meal at the dorm. I lived off campus and prepared all of my meals, but nonetheless, the free food was a treat for me also. Even though McDonald's ushered in the advent of fast food during our college years, building one of the first of its restaurants in our college town, we had no extra money, and certainly couldn't eat at a restaurant very often. This free meal at the church was a real treat, plus it was comfort food to the max—just like we had enjoyed at home.

Once I got these two services launched, I moved on, quite reluctantly, to join Wesley Foundation, which was a program

good habit plays itself out

of the Methodist Church—my new girlfriend, Karen, with the same name as my sister and who would become my best girlfriend for four years of college—had convinced me that Wesley Foundation was for me. My boyfriend attended every service with me; perhaps he didn't know there was another way to date because that is how we had dated while we were in high school. (Early training is never wasted.) Plus, we were successful in having his twin brother join us for the food on Sunday evening. Again, while this arrangement may look picture-book perfect, this was totally an act of obedience and only a few steps above drudgery on many Sundays, especially near exam time.

Now as I look at life today, I work through the idea of church attendance in this way:

Why will we attend church this Sunday? To confess to God who we think we are.

In the presence of God we come to realize a heart that is humbled by—Truth—the Holy Spirit and the Word. If we did not attend church our hearts would not be humbled and no need felt, no confession would take place.

Each week we need to admit, "I am an unworthy servant," said Hal Large missionary to El Salvador, in a sermon which explains so well why we attend church.

> • Hearing the Word of God in the house of the Lord with the Holy Spirit present, we receive something

we can get nowhere else. The experience is just like coming to the end of our rope and falling in a heap in prayer, we receive something we can get nowhere else. The Word, when heard, pierces or reveals and judges the thoughts and intents of the heart, and all is opened and laid bare in the eyes of Jesus Christ—regularly. If we don't attend, piercing (as distinguished from strong feelings) is not likely to take place.

• Also, in the act of going to the church services—we draw near to Him, so He can draw near to us and be ready to help us in the coming week in time of need.

• At church, we can more clearly see what we profess and don't practice. In daily life it is more difficult to see "the forest for the trees." From our comfortable chair in our family room at home that revelation is not likely to come to us week after week.

• We attend church in order to receive a regular cleansing so that on the day of trouble, when we enter the sickroom or enter a time of crisis, we do not go in carrying a burden of sin strapped to our backs, preventing not only having to deal with the illness, or crisis, but we also have to deal with the mountain of sin.

• We attend church in order to become transparent, to have our lives laid bare. Who would conduct such surgery on herself while enjoying the Sunday newspaper on the front porch?

good habit plays itself out

• If we decide to skip church, we miss out on hearing the testimonies of others who have been through some of the same things we are experiencing. Thus, we lose the opportunity to double our faith. How can we go from faith to faith, glory to glory, when we have nothing to feed that growth?

• We go to church to taste of the heavenly age to come — when in chorus we sing praises to God.

• We go to church to get acquainted with the power of God. We will not make room for that power while swinging in the porch swing, living our life on our own power.

• We go to church automatically — or God will bring us to church as a result of a trial — one way or the other we will see God in church.

• By church attendance the truth about what we REALLY love is exposed where it probably wouldn't be as easily revealed as we sit on the porch swing. "We love you, Lord, but we just love other things more." At church, we get healed of this thinking.

• Why attend church? I follow a risen Savior. I go to church each Sunday to offer my continuing allegiance to this risen Savior. I cannot do this at home because there must be an element of sacrifice in this endeavor.

• We attend church in order to have our senses trained so we can take on solid food. It is likely we will not go on to solid food while sitting in the park enjoying the season.

Picnic *on* the grounds

- We attend church in search of the blessings God has told us He has for us. Psalm 84:4 NIV: "Blessed are those who dwell in your house...."

- We go to church to sacrifice our morning, this precious amount of time when we could really relax and prepare for the week ahead. We give a sacrifice of praise and thanks to God for all He is and all He has done for us.

- We attend church in order to glean touchstone verses, quotes and little bits of language we can quote for the remainder of our lives, lines that mean much to us.

- We attend church when Christ is head and shun the various activities of other beliefs because we do not want to present a mixed message to the world. We believe there is only one Savior—Jesus Christ.

In addition to the well-phrased thoughts of Hal Large, here are additional thoughts on the subject:

- We attend church because we have learned "there are truly no "individual" acts" as quoted by John Koessler. The behavior of one has implications for many...I Corinthians 12:25. "A little yeast affects the whole batch of dough." I Corinthians 5:6. We are a part of the body of Christ in the world today.

- David Wilkerson of Times Square Church Pulpit Series, NYC, April 3, 1995 adds to that thought with: "It amazes me that so many people who say they are in love with Jesus come to a hard place and yet won't turn to

good habit plays itself out

him. Why won't we shut ourselves into His presence and pour out our hearts to Him?

• He continues, "You may answer: 'I'm just not in the habit of doing that. I'm not much of a praying person. Instead of going to God, I carry the whole load myself.'"

• David of the Old Testament of the Bible shows us that running to God in time of trouble was his secret. He cried out, "Deliver me, O Lord, from mine enemies: I flee unto thee to hide me." Psalm 143:9.

• David would agree with the principle of running toward God by running to his place of meeting, the church, when he said, "…bring me unto thy holy hill, and to thy tabernacles. Then will I go unto the altar of God, unto God my exceeding joy." Psalm 43:3-4.

• I attend church services, for I have learned that "God may channel my blessings through several of his people before those blessings actually reach me. And where do I find His people congregated? At church. Therefore, I need to be where the people of God meet, where blessings are often dispensed. Plus, after reading His Word, I have learned that God expects all of that of me.

• I attend church services so that I will not be left with the problem of trying to reconcile Ephesians 5:32-33 KJV, if I do not attend: *This is a great mystery: but I speak concerning Christ and the church.*

What happens when one physically walks through the doorway of a church building? I recall one church service, described in my book *A Whirlwind's Breath*, when the answers I needed, I received:

CHRISTMAS EVE

One month after the diagnosis of Brian's brain tumor, we attended Christmas Eve services at church. Pastor David Powell read from Luke 1:26-56. The passage begins with "Greetings, you are highly favored! The Lord is with you." Mary was greatly troubled..." Then the passage ends with Mary's song of joy.

Very receptive, hanging on to every word, I heard "highly favored," "greatly troubled," and "song of joy"—conflicting words, yet used together. I knew there was a message for me on the Christmas with one son's leukemia in remission and one son's brain tumor under observation "to see if it changes." On the one hand, I had the wonderful joy of Christmas and all that goes with Christmas, and on the other hand I was terrified.

In *A Whirlwind's Breath*, I continued:

...Anyone who lives with a chronic illness or a terminal prognosis will agree that the most difficult days are those in which the most wonderful and the most feared take up residence in the same mind. Praise be to God that Mary's song of joy resolves that dilemma for all of us, for it is more than O.K. to be faithful and afraid at the same time. In spite of Mary's fears, God chose her to be the mother of Jesus.

good habit plays itself out

To remind me of that often faithful yet fearful feeling, I have a painting in my hallway of the boarding of the animals—two by two—as they walked up the plank to come on board with Noah. This painting caught my eye because of the fearful look in the eyes of each animal—that wild, woolly look of knowing the rains were coming, sensing it in the way only the animal kingdom can, and yet obediently boarding this man-made ark; fearful, yet obedient.

You've told Jesus that you believe He did for you what He said He would. You have confessed that you are sorry for all of the times when you have gone your own way completely ignoring Him. You feel that God has accepted that confession and that your destiny for eternal life is assured.

You live a moral life; take care of your family; do not hold prejudiced views and would never cheat someone of what is his alone. Your religion is a private one. You find closeness to God when you have a quiet moment or when you are alone on the golf course. You often listen to Christian tapes, read testimonies of Christian writers. You understand the differences between the denominations and the varieties of beliefs about such things as baptism, communion, etc. Hearing the hymns of faith can move you greatly. Yet, even with all of the truths presented by these carriers of the Word, you continue to say, "So why with all of my Christian maturity would it be necessary for me to go to a church, come under the guidance of the church's leadership, and come into unity with God's people?

Journal Reflections on Chapter 5:

1. While my "regular church attendance is a good habit" sounds more like what I did for 12 years on my own power and not with God's help, what merit do you see in espousing that habit when a person doesn't quite know what to do?

2. If you drew a time line of your church experience, putting in the highs and lows, what would it look like?

3. Why is it so difficult to leave a church family to become a part of another?

4. Of the reasons I have listed for church attendance, which do you most identify with?

5. What do you learn about church attendance from Psalm 84?

6. Why would a person come to a difficult place in life and not turn to the church family for help?

7. Have you ever processed events in which the most wonderful and the most sorrowful go hand in hand?

Chapter 6

At Church We See What His Sacrifice Is and What Ours Is

The second incident that clarified for me why I must attend church services, become a part of the body of Christ, and serve Him through the organized church came one evening in the early 1990s as I taught an evening college class.

On this particular evening I was returning pages from journal keeping the students had submitted the week before. This journal was merely a recounting of the events of the week,

Picnic on the grounds

making the writing more than a diary account, but rather a journal entry in which the student focused on one thought from the day and expounded upon it. The entry that I will forever remember was submitted by a student who was the same age as one of my own sons. This student, because of what he learned and what he taught me, is memorable indeed. He had an athletic, football player frame, dark hair and had a congenial manner. His interests ran along the lines of an outdoors man—fisherman, hunter, trapper. His journal entry for the previous Sunday read like this:

Sunday—Today is a day of rest and to go to church. I don't rest and I don't go to church. The way I figure it, God's in my house as well as in church. I can be with Him at home. So on Sundays I stay home, take walks in the woods and commune with nature. Since I feel his presence there, I don't need the church.

At the next class meeting as I returned the journal pages, I watched to see his expression when he read my comment to this particular entry. Slowly, he turned the pages, almost every page had a comment on it, some in agreement, some humorous, but all related to what he had written on that page. Finally, he turned to the Sunday entry and began to read. Totally lost in what he was reading and totally unaware that he was being observed, he turned pale and became very quiet and thoughtful and remained so for the remainder of the class time.

what his sacrifice is

Later he told my son,

"Your mother—she nailed me."

"Oh, really. What did she do?"

"Well, I had written an explanation of how I spend my Sundays—at home and not attending church. Then I explained that I could feel close to God while enjoying my down time as well as I could in church. And do you know what she wrote on my paper?"

"No, but I think I might be able to guess the drift of what she wrote."

The boy laughed and said, "She wrote four words that I will never forget. Your mother wrote, 'Where is the sacrifice?'"

"Ya, she nailed me!"

Well, more than a decade has passed since this incident, and I will always remember how I came to write those four words. Obviously the object of this particular class was not to convince students regarding how they should utilize their Sundays. Yet, I knew the words I wrote would be thought provoking, and that was an objective of the class. The simplicity and direct phrasing were not my own. I heard the words as clearly as if someone were in the room and speaking them.

"Sacrifice? Where is the sacrifice?"

Picnic *on* the grounds

Wow! "Where IS the sacrifice?" Of course—sacrifice—that was part of the answer. Sacrifice was a key element in the importance of physically walking through a church door on Sunday morning in order to worship God.

What is more cherished than a Sunday morning with no commitments? Lazily whiling away the time while others are preoccupied with church or their own whiling away? Reading the Sunday newspaper while the news is fresh and not reading it some time next week when you finally have time for the extra reading? Enjoying a cup of coffee without having to dump half of it down the sink because you have to hurry off on an errand or to attend a church service? Even having a moment to enjoy the sounds of solitude? Or to have a completely, uninterrupted thought?

To give all of that up…to willfully walk away from such pleasure, that is indeed a sacrifice. That is part of what God meant when the Scripture said, " …offer to God a sacrifice of praise."

Now I had two parts of the equation—church attendance is a practice smiled upon by God, our Creator, because He knows we form habits and need the truths as perimeters for daily living and, because we who believe in Jesus Christ offer him a sacrifice of praise at the worship service at church.

Journal Reflections in Chapter 6:

1. What is the sacrifice of praise that you bring to the church service this week?

2. What would you do with the hours when church services are held if you did not attend church?

3. Besides feeling close to God while in church services, where and when do you feel close to Him?

CHAPTER 7

At the Picnic on the Grounds, in Relationship, We See God in It All

The day when, out of pure obedience, church attendance becomes more than a physical act of "darkening a door" and finding a seat—Jesus finds us and we find Him. When we seek Him by running toward Him rather than running away from Him, the day will come when we will no longer ask, "If Jesus paid it all in those early days, why do I need to attend church now?"

Through the ages, those who have carried the Gospel even into the most remote areas of the world, point to the importance of having a relationship with Jesus. In fact, our

Picnic on the grounds

purpose for living—glorifying God and enjoying Him forever, cannot be accomplished without our having formed a relationship with God.

For me, the sharpest and most memorable picture of our relationship with Jesus comes from seeing the sacrament of marriage interspersed throughout the continuing story of the Scriptures from Genesis to Revelation.

Even though I had read Ephesians 5:25-27 (Husbands love your wives, just as Christ loved the church and gave Himself up for her to make her holy, cleansing her by the washing with water through the Word, and to present her to Himself as a radiant church, without stain or wrinkle or any other blemish, but holy and blameless.) I did not really understand what it meant.

When a slight glimmering of understanding presented itself, I began to understand more about the institution of marriage. From Genesis on, I noted the genius of how God wove together the metaphor of marriage between man and woman and the metaphor of Jesus as bridegroom and the church as bride. Let me retrace some of what I found as those metaphors continued reappearing from Genesis 1 to Revelation's end.

In Genesis, we see that God knew man was lonely. The animals he had created, that surrounded man, did not take away his loneliness (Genesis 2:19). Therefore, God extracted from

we see God in it all

Adam's side, from his rib, the perfect mate—a woman who would be his companion and take away his loneliness. Right there on the page, a deeper meaning unfolded. Eve was taken from the side of man, literally creating a wound, which God immediately healed. The church was taken from the deep spear wound of Jesus Christ as He died on the cross.

Moving on, we have the Creation story and no sooner have we heard the final "And God saw that it was good," then God institutes the sacrament of marriage. Man would leave his father and mother, take a wife and the two would become one. (Genesis 2:24) Jesus and the church shall become one, thus we get the phrase, Body of Christ (Ephesians 5:23).

The relationship of man and woman reappears in the stories of Abraham and Sarah, Isaac and Rebekah, Jacob and Rachel, David and Bathsheba, Boaz and Ruth and the story continues.

Furthermore, two books of the Old Testament, Song of Solomon and Hosea, specifically discuss God's view of the sexual intimacy of marriage and the sorrow of unfaithfulness. In both of these books, there is also the metaphor of Jesus and his people, the church. The words say, "you know how a man loves a woman," and the metaphor says that's how completely Jesus loves the church. He died for her.

Skipping over the Gospels and into the book of Acts, we see the first Christian church organized, and the church movement spread throughout the known world. With the enthusiastic and committed Apostle Paul leading this movement, how could it not spread? God chose the man to lead the church movement and then worked through him.

Even in the final book of the Bible, Revelation, the metaphor of Christ loving the church as a husband loves a wife continues in Chapter 2 when God tells the Apostle John to write down what God thinks of seven well-known churches of the time. In his reply we find God calling the churches, God's people, to return to their first love—to Him—for He longs to be in close relationship with them.

And finally we come to the wedding of Jesus and the church described in Revelation, Jesus, the knight in shining armor coming out of the clouds to whisk His bride, the church away.

Revelation 19:6b-9 An angel is speaking:

> "Hallelujah! For our Lord God Almighty reigns.
> Let us rejoice and be glad and give Him glory!
> For the wedding of the Lamb has come,
> And His bride has made herself ready.
> Fine linen, bright and clean, was given her to wear."

> Then the angel said to me,

> "Write: Blessed are those who are invited
> To the wedding supper of the Lamb!"

> And he added, "These are the true words of God."

we see God in it all

We have the picture of the bride in her chamber carefully preparing herself, something borrowed, something blue—veil and white gown and all, for her groom who will soon see her coming down the aisle to meet him. She will not be late, unlovely or unprepared.

She will come to meet him, perfect in every way. And he meets her, escorts her to the wedding supper and then carries her away "til death do they part."

In the same manner, suddenly the doors of heaven are opened and Jesus, riding on a white horse, thunders out of the clouds to go to the wedding feast. His bride, the church, is there to meet Him, an appointment the bride will not miss. She will not be late. She will be clean from all wrong because she has taken on the righteousness He gave her at the cross, blameless in every way. Dressed in pure white, she will meet Him, He will escort her to the wedding supper and then carry her away to be God's heiress with Him forever and ever.

The bottom line: Jesus, the bridegroom loves His bride, the church just as husbands are to love their wives.

In his book *Secrets of the Secret Place*, Bob Sorge writes, "The bridal imagery of a cosmic wedding appears frequently throughout the entire Bible….Believers fulfill the feminine role in the relationship as we commune with our Lord. He initiates, we respond; He gives, we receive; He impregnates, we bring to birth; He leads, we follow; He loves, we reciprocate; He rules, we reign with Him....We relate to the Father as sons, we relate to the Lord Jesus as a bride."

Sorge continues, "It's true that we're soldiers, and we are involved in high-level strategic warfare, and the Lord is depending on us to fight the good fight of faith. And it's true that we're laborers in His vineyard, working assiduously in the harvest fields to bring all of the wheat into His barn. But Jesus didn't die to win for Himself an army or a labor force; He died for a bride. We don't come to the secret place as a soldier looking for battle plans...nor do we come as laborers looking to gain strength for the day's labors, even though He will strengthen us for the tasks before us. We come primarily as His bride, to enjoy His embrace and to lavish upon Him our love. The secret place is a celebration of our highest identity—His bride! It's the place of the intimate love exchange."

The day I really understood that metaphor—that union—was the day I knew how precious is the marriage of a woman and a man, and even more precious is the union of Jesus to his people—the church. Breaking trust in either area surely causes Jesus to weep as he did over the city of Jerusalem just before he died for her.

We ARE the bride.

Whiling the time away on the golf course, picking up shells at the beach, lounging away the morning hours at home,

we see God in it all

when we know there is a meeting of God's people held at that same hour seems incongruous with the revelation we have just heard. If there's a meeting of God's people somewhere nearby—I want to be there! I am the bride. Jesus, who died for me, is returning for me someday. I do not want to miss the wedding supper (Rev. 19:9).

We come to meet our groom offering the sacrifice of our Sunday morning leisure hours as we enter the sanctuary, the meeting house. We come into His presence adorned for Him, wearing His righteousness, not our own, thereby acknowledging to Him that we know we live and breathe because He has made it possible.

Jesus said, "Wherever two or three are gathered together, I will be there in their midst." (Matthew 18:20) We know not to question that; we believe it. Therefore, we head out to meet Him in the meeting house, the church. And so, in essence—the picnic on the grounds of the church is the reaping of the benefits of church attendance. It is at church, where we are gathered together that we see there are miracles of health, nature, and provision occurring all around us. As a result of what we hear from our brothers and sisters, our faith, that fragile flame that has often threatened to go out, grows. We move from faith unto faith, like one skipping over the stones in the creek bed. Yet our leaping from faith to faith is not linear—sometimes it seems there is no pattern to it at all, but most often the leaping is like moving up rungs of a ladder, ever going higher and higher. As a result of that

Picnic *on* the grounds

growing faith, when the day comes, that day we have dreaded all of our lives, when all appears to be lost, we have a powerful force to hold on to.

That day—you know which day I am discussing. That day, in my own household lasted for fifteen years, as day after day we feared we would lose one or both of our children—first to leukemia and then to a brain tumor. A fifteen-year-long-day makes a strong impression.

The following is the best description I have ever read of that day.

Standing face to face with the end of the universe.

Written by Bruce Hetrick, author of the Not Strictly Business column for the *Indianapolis Business Journal*, March 1-7, 2004.

"...He tells me there's a problem.

He tells me that even after surgery to remove tumors, nerves, lymph nodes and muscle tissue from Pam's neck; even after jolts of radiation to stifle any cancer left behind; even after a positron emission tomography (PET) scan that found no cancer anywhere else, the CT scan shows a few tiny lesions on both of Pam's lungs.

And he tells me they can't safely operate on them.

And he tells me they can't safely radiate them.

And he tells me chemotherapy has a lousy cure rate for this kind of cancer.

we see God in it all

And by the time he's finished, I'm lying on the floor, because my eyes are clouding and my ears are roaring; and Einstein with his big rips and big crunches, and Frost with his ice and fire, and all the scientists with their forecasts of oblivion tens of billions of years from now are all wrong because oblivion is here, at this moment, on this industrial carpet, in this ever-shrinking room for educational purposes ONLY.

And then it gets worse.

Because we have to tell Pam.

We have to tell her that even after she's downed her doses of radioactive Kool-Aid, and lain stock-still on scanning devices, and had needles poked in her lymph nodes, and suffered a serious surgery, and had radiation shot into the open wound and had the whole thing stapled shut, this blasted, baneful, cursed, execrable, infernal, damnable disease isn't gone. It's still inside her. Hatching its hideous cells. And the physicians are telling us they can't kill it...."

While there is still breath to breathe, it is never too late to begin the journey from faith to faith in the understanding of what Jesus has done for us and what he has promised he will do for us. While there is life, it is never too late to become an arm or a leg of the body of Christ—the church.

Like the thoroughbred horse that looks straight ahead as it runs toward the prize, not looking at the motley crowd that might distract it, a prospective church member steps out and

Picnic *on* the grounds

joins the wedding party, the picnic, the rewarding moment, led by the groom who knows everything and who owns it all. Settling for anything less means settling for answers found with the resources of this limited world, answers that will have little worth on **that** day, like the one described by Bruce Hetrick, or any other fractured day in this often troubled world.

In the late years of the 19th and the early years of the 20th centuries, the churches often planned to have the special picnic on the grounds. In the 1950s I attended these events held at a rural church in Southern Indiana. To the side of the church building, the men of the church had constructed a permanent picnic table among the trees on the grove. The table's boards were all of 2 inches thick, with supports and braces in the underpinnings lest the food weigh the table into a dip. At the side of this table women opened baskets and boxes of the fruit of their best skills—platters of fried chicken like few have eaten today, tall cakes with filling between the layers and covered with coconut, bowl after bowl, plate after plate with few duplicates, all placed on a 24 foot long table. At each end of the table were large containers of sugared iced tea and lemonade. After the blessing on the food, no one appeared to exercise restraint in food choices, for no one knew there were carbs hiding in the food, that sugar could kill them, or the fat was lurking in the fried chicken. No, it was the ultimate feast—maybe a picture of the future wedding supper of the Lamb—the celebration of the reunion of Jesus and us made whole forever in heaven. While temporal, the picnic became a picture of the beginning of the reward for choosing to be in the body of Christ.

we see God in it all

There are many and varied versions of that picnic on the grounds. We were celebrating that picnic as I wrote in our Christmas letter of 2004. Note that what I allude to here—I had recently learned while in church.

December 2004:

One year we decided to add the color of straw to our Christmas décor-little bales of straw, straw-colored ribbon, binder twine. Outside we had fresh straw-colored mulch around the trees and artificial poinsettias, and even left the ornamental grass blowing in the breeze—when really it was supposed to be cut down in the fall. Yes, we were on a straw kick—so pretty with true red and green—and so appropriate for remembering the manger.

Well, this Christmas we are on a white kick—white added to the Christmas décor. This was brought about because of the sermons of Advent at church. We are the bride—the bridegroom was born on Christmas day. So—this year we have tufts of white lace stuffed into greenery throughout. Yards of white lace in the banister swag. Jesus and his bride! Not a bad thought to carry one through the rough spots of life....

Yes the ones who choose to be a part of the body of Christ are reaping the rewards of church attendance. They are surrounded by the love and prayers of people of one mind—even in their differences—who share an understanding about who the Savior is.

Picnic *on* the grounds

A close look at two of the old hymns of the church could illuminate, could give an understanding of what Jesus meant when he said the church is his bride. What does it mean to be the bride of Jesus Christ?

O Master, Let Me Walk With Thee
Washington Gladden • Arranged by Robert Schumann

O Master, let me walk with Thee
In lowly paths of service free;
Tell me thy secret;
Help me bear,
The strain of toil,
The fret of care.

Help me the slow of heart to move
By some clear, winning word of love;
Teach me the wayward feet to stay,
And guide them in the homeward way.

Teach me thy patience;
Still with Thee
In closer, dearer company,
In work that keeps faith sweet and strong,
In trust that triumphs over wrong.

In hope that sends a shining ray
Far down the future's broad'ning way;
In peace that only Thou canst give,
With Thee, O Master, let me live.

we see God in it all

The Church's One Foundation
Samuel J. Stone • Samuel S. Wesley

The church's one foundation
Is Jesus Christ her Lord;
She is His new creation
By water and the word:
From heaven He came and sought her
To be His holy bride;
With His own blood He bought her,
And for her life He died.

Elect from every nation,
Yet one o'er all the earth,
Her charter of salvation,
One Lord, one faith, one birth;
One holy name she blesses,
Partakes one holy food,
And to one hope she presses,
With every grace endued.

'Mid toil and tribulation,
And tumult of her war,
She waits the consummation
Of peace forevermore;
Till with the vision glorious,
Her longing eyes are blest,
And the great church victorious
Shall be the church at rest.

Picnic *on* the grounds

Yet she on earth hath union
With God the Three in One,
And mystic sweet communion
With those whose rest is won:
O happy ones and holy!
Lord, give us grace that we
Like them, the meek and lowly,
On high may dwell with Thee.

Journal Reflections in Chapter 7:

1. If Jesus paid it all in those days of old, why do I attend church services now?

2. What do you learn from the analogy of husbands loving their wives like Jesus loved the church?

3. How does this analogy affect your view of marriage and divorce?

4. Do you see the parallel in the preparations a modern day bride makes and the preparations the bride of Christ makes for that day when Jesus comes for her?

5. God likes to hear the prayers of two or three gathered together. How is the power of prayer multiplied when that prayer is offered in church by the entire body?

6. What was your reaction to the Bruce Hetrick description of the day when the man and his wife received the doctor's diagnosis and prognosis?

Scripture References Regarding the Church and Us:

Deuteronomy 14:2 .... Family of God
Deuteronomy 14:22-26 .... Church dinners
Judges 2:10 .... Generation away from possible extinction
Psalm 84:4 .... Place of blessing
Isaiah 11:10 KJV .... Prophet's vision
Isaiah 37:1 .... Place of refuge
Isaiah 37:14 .... Search for wisdom
Micah 4:2 .... Church for all nations
Matthew 12:9, Mark 1:21 .... Jesus' frequent attendance
Matthew 16:18 .... Divinely instituted church
Matthew 18:17 .... Recognition by Jesus
Matthew 22:1-14 .... Many invited to the wedding banquet
Luke 2:36-37; Luke 24:52-53 .... Daily attendance
Luke 4:16 .... Childhood pattern
Luke 18:10 .... Varied congregational membership
John 17:20-23 .... Prayer of Jesus for his own
John 18:36 .... Kingdom not of this world

Picnic *on* the grounds

John 19:26-27	New relationships in Christ
Acts 15:13-21, Acts 18:6	Message to the Gentiles
Acts 16:5	Strong churches winning converts
Romans 12:4-8	The parts of the church
Romans 15:5-6	Unity in serving together
Romans 16:5	Special greeting to house church
I Corinthians 5:6	Boasting about church
I Corinthians 12:4-11	Gifts of the people in the church
I Corinthians 12: 12-20	One body, many parts
Galatians 6:2,5	Carry one another's burdens
Galatians 6:10	Relationships within the fold
Ephesians 1:9-10; Ephesians 3:2-3	Church is a mystery
Ephesians 2:19-20; I Timothy 3:15	God's household
Ephesians 2:22	Dwelling place for God
Ephesians 4:3	Unity
Ephesians 4: 11-13	Varied talents in the body
Ephesians 5:1-2	Imitators of God in expressing love to others
Ephesians 5:19-20	Conduct in worship
Ephesians 6:19-20	Pray for minister
Philippians 1:27-28	United for a singular purpose
Philippians 2:1-2	Like-minded people serving in love
Philippians 3:20	Spiritual commonwealth
I Timothy 3:15	Truth pillar
I Timothy 4:13	Public Scripture reading
I Timothy 5:1-2	Christian community is a family
I Timothy 6:12	Convert's public testimony

scripture references

Titus 1:1-3	Promised from time's beginning
Titus 1:5-9	Needs of new congregation
Titus 2:1-10	Proper teaching for all ages
Hebrews 2:12	Singing
Hebrews 3:13	Encouraging one another
Hebrews 6:9	Growth in followers
Hebrews 10:25	Admonition to attend worship
Hebrews 13:1	Brotherly love
James 2:1-4	Hospitality to all
I Peter 1:22; I John 4:7-11	Love one another deeply
I Peter 2:5	Living stones
I John 2:12-14	Message for all ages
Revelation 2:29	Holy Spirit speaks to the churches
Revelation 14:1-3	Song for congregation
Revelation 21:22	No churches in heaven
Revelation 22:17	Ministry of Holy Spirit in church in evangelism

Works Cited

Chatham, Judith McCart, *A Whirlwind's Breath*, Guild Press of Indiana, Zionsville, Indiana, 1998.

Hetrick, Bruce, "Standing Face to Face with the End of the Universe," *Indianapolis Business Journal*, March 1-7, 2004.

Large, Hal, Missionary to El Salvador, Speaking at a Mission's Conference in Greenwood, Indiana, 2002.

Sorge, Bob, *Secrets of the Secret Place*, Oasis House, Lee's Summit, Missouri, 2001.

Wilkerson, David, *Times Square Church Pulpit Series*, Times Square Church, New York City, New York, January 2004.